The Sayings

The Sayings Series
*Jane Austen
Brendan Behan
Charlotte Brontë
Lord Byron
Lewis Carroll
Winston Churchill
Noel Coward
Charles Dickens
Benjamin Disraeli
F. Scott Fitzgerald
Benjamin Franklin
Goethe
Thomas Hardy
Henrik Ibsen
Dr Johnson
James Joyce
John Keats
Rudyard Kipling
D.H. Lawrence
Somerset Maugham
Friedrich Nietzsche
George Orwell
Dorothy Parker
Samuel Pepys
Ezra Pound
Sir Walter Scott
William Shakespeare
George Bernard Shaw
Sydney Smith
R.L. Stevenson
Jonathan Swift
Leo Tolstoy
Anthony Trollope
Mark Twain
Evelyn Waugh
Oscar Wilde
Virginia Woolf
William Wordsworth
W.B. Yeats
The Bible
The Buddha
Jesus
Moses
Muhammad*

The Sayings of

BRENDAN
BEHAN

edited by
Aubrey Dillon-Malone

DUCKWORTH

First published in 1997 by
Gerald Duckworth & Co. Ltd.
The Old Piano Factory
48 Hoxton Square, London N1 6PB
Tel: 0171 729 5986
Fax: 0171 729 0015

Introduction and editorial arrangement
© 1997 by Aubrey Dillon-Malone
Quotations from the works of Brendan Behan
© The Estate of Brendan Behan.

The editor and publisher are grateful to The Tessa Sayle Agency for permission to quote from *Brendan Behan's New York*, *The Hostage* and *Richard's Cork Leg*, and to Random House UK for permission to quote from *Hold Your Hour and Have Another*, *Borstal Boy*, *Confessions of an Irish Rebel* and *Brendan Behan's Island*.
   The quotation from *Vogue* is © Conde Nast /British Vogue

Every effort has been made to trace copyright holders of material printed in this book. The editor and publisher will be glad to hear from anyone who has inadvertently not been consulted.

All rights reserved. No part of this publication
may be reproduced, stored in a retrieval system, or
transmitted, in any form or by any means, electronic,
mechanical, photocopying, recording or otherwise,
without the prior permission of the publisher.

A catalogue record for this book is available
from the British Library

ISBN 0 7156 2806 2

Typeset by Ray Davies
Printed in Great Britain by
Redwood Books Ltd, Trowbridge

Contents

7	Introduction
19	Behan on Behan
23	Behan on Others
25	Writers & Writing
31	Ireland & the Irish
35	Other Nationalities
40	Alcohol
44	Fame & the Media
46	Religion
51	Insults
56	Money
57	Wit
59	Violence
61	General Ruminations

Sources

Primary

The Hostage, Methuen 1958.
Borstal Boy, Hutchinson 1959.
Brendan Behan's Island, Hutchinson 1962.
Hold Your Hour and Have Another, Hutchinson 1963.
Brendan Behan's New York, Hutchinson 1964.
Confessions of an Irish Rebel, Hutchinson 1965.
Richard's Cork Leg, Methuen 1973.

Secondary

The World of Brendan Behan, ed. Sean McCann, New English Library 1965.
My Brother Brendan by Dominic Behan, Leslie Frewen 1965.
Man and Showman by Rae Jeffs, Hutchinson 1966.
The Wit of Brendan Behan, ed. Sean McCann, Leslie Frewen 1968.
Brendan Behan by Ted Boyle, Twayne 1969.
Brendan Behan by Ulick O'Connor, Hamish Hamilton 1970 [all references to this title are to this book unless otherwise indicated].
A Paler Shade of Green by Gus Smith, Leslie Frewen 1972.
My Life With Brendan by Beatrice Behan, Leslie Frewen 1973.
Dead as Doornails by Anthony Cronin, Dolmen 1976.
With Brendan Behan by Peter Arthurs, St Martin's Press 1981.
Interviews and Recollections ed. E.H. Mikhail, Macmillan 1982.
Me Darlin' Dublin's Dead and Gone by Bill Kelly, Pollbeg 1983.
A Memoir by Seamus de Burca, Proscenium 1985.
Remembering How We Stood by John Ryan, Lilliput 1987.
More Kicks than Pence by Michael O'Toole, Poolbeg 1992.
The Real Keane by Gus Smith and Des Hickey, Poolbeg 1992.
Smile and Be a Villain by Niall Toibin, Town House 1995.

Introduction

If Brendan Behan hasn't been accorded the critical acclaim he deserves in the thirty odd years since his demise, part of the fault must lie in himself, because he spent most of his short life either trivialising his work or marginalising it, having had his soul hijacked by the media men and the publishing trade, and his personality seduced by the hangers-on and the trappings of a fame – or rather infamy – he was always too wayward to appreciate properly. He did, however, cram more living into his 41 years than most people manage in double that time, so perhaps his tragedy isn't as great as it might have been in a more rarefied or frugal temperament.

He started life in a tenement household in Dublin on the 9 February 1923, the eldest of seven children born to Stephen and Kathleen Behan. His origins weren't as proletarian as he would subsequently make out, however. His grandfather on his father's side had been a painting contractor, and his mother's family had been well-to-do farmers. Her grandmother had much property, including the house in Russell Street where he lived, rent-free, until they moved out to Crumlin.

There was much singing and dancing done in the Behan home, and both his parents were inveterate theatre-goers. A painter by trade, Stephen was almost as colourful a character as his son would eventually turn out to be – as, indeed, was Kathleen, who had been married before and widowed, bringing two sons with her into her marriage to Stephen.

Brendan was a rumbustious lad almost from birth. By the age of three he was reading, by six he could recite Robert Emmet's 'Speech From the Dock', by nine he was writing letters to his friends in verse, and three years later he was having articles printed in newspapers. His behaviour in class left something to be desired, however. Educated (if that's the word) by the French Sisters of Charity (Sister Monica realised early on that she had a genius of sorts on her hands) he spent three years afterwards with the Christian Brothers, but he had no great love for school, nor school for him, and it wasn't long before he left it to follow his father's footsteps and become a painter too.

Stephen was a staunch nationalist and had been imprisoned for revolutionary activities towards the end of the Civil War. Brendan inherited these republican ideals and at the age of fourteen joined Fianna Eireann, the youth organisation of the IRA. Two years later he was arrested in Liverpool for the possession of explosives. This was not a formal IRA operation and it's likely Behan was sent on it as much to get him out of Ireland – where he was deemed to be a security risk due to his garrulousness – as to do any damage in Britain. As a result of it, in any case, he was sentenced to three years in borstal, the maximum that could be given to a juvenile. Behan was just one day off his seventeenth birthday when he was sent down. With the exception of six months, he would spend all of his time from the age of 16 to 22 behind bars.

In April 1942, at a parade in Glasnevin Cemetery to commemorate the Easter Rising of 1916, he fired a couple of shots at a detective and was caught after a few days. He was sentenced to fourteen years penal servitude for this offence, and was lucky it wasn't life. As things worked out, he was released after serving only four years of his sentence, due to a post-war amnesty. He later quipped, in a self-deprecatory tone that was to become his trademark, 'Anyone who misses a target at 14 yards, deserves a year in prison for every yard.'

Ironically enough, in years to come he would become a drinking partner of Paddy Donegan, the plainclothes policeman he had tried to shoot. Such a rendezvous transpired when Behan had softened in his republican stance, and when he seemed content to dramatise the events of his youth from the mellow perspective of the successful scribe who looked back on his adolescent japes with something less than anger. 'The judge who sentenced me to 14 years,' he would later boast, 'sent me an electric coffee-pot as a wedding present.'

The same judge, of course, whether wittingly or not, turned Behan from republican activist to budding scribe with that pound of the gavel, for while he was in prison he developed a great love of reading (particularly books written in Irish) and also fine-tuned his budding writing talent. Prison, in addition, gave him a sense of discipline that was markedly absent in his life before and since – with the possible exception of the early years of his marriage. And of course prison perforce kept him away from drink, a notable achievement in itself.

After his release, he continued to support 'The Cause', and in 1947 he travelled to England with a false passport in a ludicrous attempt to spring a fellow IRA man from prison. He was arrested shortly after his arrival just as he was arrested after the zany trip to Liverpool at the age of sixteen, or after the equally botched shooting incident in de Courcey Square in 1942. In fact one wonders if Behan ever *successfully* negotiated an IRA mission. He said himself that the organisation showed great *savoir faire* in never elevating him beyond the rank of courier, a sentiment underlined by Sean Kavanaugh, the Governor of Mountjoy Jail, who said after Behan's arrival there: 'Meeting this mild-mannered boy gave one a feeling of anti-climax; surely this was no desperado, no trigger-happy gunman. ... The better one grew to know him, the more the impression grew that basically he was a very gentle person who in his senses would not hurt a fly.'

Out of prison and with as huge an appetite for self-publicity as he had for the writing craft, he had numerous articles and poems published in various literary magazines such as *The Bell*, and also became something of a man-about-town as he regaled all and sundry with colourful tales of his time in 'the pokey' and other miscellaneous anecdotes. But it wasn't until 1954, and the production of his play *The Quare Fellow* in the Pike Theatre, that he became a household name for the literati. It was subsequently moved to London, thus garnering him the beginning of his international fame, a fame that would be based

Introduction

as much on his drunken antics as his writing ability, if not more so.

Behan spent the next few years involved in various pursuits – painting, travelling, brawling, etc. – the only unifying thread being the ubiquitous presence of alcohol. He also did some stretches in prison, one of which was for assaulting a policeman (the sight of his uniform, he explained, distressed him). He also worked as a freelance journalist for the *Irish Press*, a newspaper to which he contributed 'slice of life' articles that would subsequently be published in book form as *Hold Your Hour and Have Another*.

In 1953 Behan published a slight novel, *The Scarperer*, under the pseudonym 'Emmett Street' and a year later *The Quare Fellow* was staged. During a performance of this he met the woman who was to become his wife, Beatrice Salkeld. The daughter of a well-known artist, Cecil ffrench-Salkeld, she had a refined personality and Behan was immediately smitten by her. They were married in February 1955, but Behan didn't tell his family about the wedding until afterwards, for fear they would think he had somehow betrayed his working class origins by choosing this effete Mona Lisa. Beatrice, for her part, had no problem. 'I didn't marry you because you were respectable,' she said later, 'I married you because I liked you.' While many felt it was a liaison doomed to disaster, the chemistry produced by his ribaldry and her sweetness seemed to gel. Beatrice also gave Behan a modicum of stability in his life that he sorely needed, and when he wasn't over-imbibing (a rare enough occurrence, admittedly) they lived a normal suburban married life.

The Quare Fellow opened in East London in 1956 and Behan, who had been banned from Britain since 1939, now found himself warmly welcomed to the country that had had such a vexed relationship with him heretofore. He followed it with *An Giall* in 1958, which was subsequently translated into English as *The Hostage*. This had run not only in Britain and Paris but also New York. 1958 also saw the publication of *Borstal Boy*, a spirited recreation of the years of his incarceration.

Much of the credit for the success of *The Hostage* has been put down to Joan Littlewood's expert direction of the play, and her unfailing antennae for what parts of it ought to have been excised or re-worked. As one of Behan's friends quipped after it was staged: 'The difference between Brendan Behan and Dylan Thomas is that Dylan wrote *Under Milk Wood* and Brendan wrote under Littlewood.'

By this stage of his life, Behan was also a broadcaster of some note, and a fairly frequent, if unpredictable, guest on television programmes. Such slots he milked to the full for the opportunities they provided him to sound off on anything that caught his fancy, ranging from literature to alcohol to casual witticisms delivered in a throwaway Oscar Wilde manner to the delight of all his listeners. In some of these appearances he was barely comprehensible due to the effect of drink; hosts realised they were skating close to the wind in inviting him to appear, but most of them felt the risk was worth it.

He continued to be the toast of both Ireland and the USA but the strain of such appearances was beginning to tell on him. Apparently undressed without a drink in his hand, he became a brilliant if abrasive raconteur, and also something of a song-and-dance man in pubs, but seemed to get into fights at the drop of a hat. He was also suffering from diabetes, which exacerbated his increasing alcoholic tendencies. Many bouts of hospitalisation followed, most due to drink-related illnesses and accidents, and even the dogs on the street knew that 'the quare fella' had become a victim of his own mini-legend.

His behaviour in theatres also became erratic, and he wasn't averse to stopping productions of his plays in mid-flow to tell the actors exactly what he thought of them. Such behaviour had a novelty value for a while, but eventually people tired of it – and him.

In his latter years, as he told Arthur Miller when they met in New York not long before he died, he wasn't so much a writer as a talker. Unable to confine himself to the rigours of sitting himself down behind a desk as he had done before drink had completely taken over his life (though it was never very far away from doing so – he had supped his first at the tender age of six) he now dictated texts into tape-recorders largely under the instigation of his friend and publisher Rae Jeffs.

Behan's tape-recorded books were *Brendan Behan's Island*, a wry collection of reflections about Ireland, *Brendan Behan's New York*, a similarly affectionate tangled skein of ruminations on things American, and *Confessions of an Irish Rebel*.

Perhaps it was fitting that such a basically bardic talent as his should eventually transmute some of those verbal gems onto the printed page in the most direct manner possible. Maybe he had been doing it all his life anyway, channelling the *bon mots* of last night's pub scene into the mouths of his theatrical personae. The pity was that the reason for this latest shift in his writing career was coming about as a result of laziness and ill health rather than a consciously self-motivated act. Rae Jeffs wasn't complaining, however, accepting the fact that Behan on auto-pilot was better than no Behan at all. And the world agreed, notwithstanding the lightweight nature of the recorded books and their occasional sloppiness.

As the drink gained on him he used any excuse not to write; any hint of a play opening abroad was sufficient temptation to draw him away from his typewriter. In a sense, New York became like a macrocosm of Dublin to him, and in no time at all he became as well known to the denizens of that city as he was to Northside Dubliners – for better or worse.

As he began to get barred from more and more pubs, Beatrice lost her hold on him and he took to staying with friends, or at his parent's house, after his binges. Anywhere there was a bed would suffice. And then the next morning he could trundle down to the nearest watering-hole for 'the cure'.

He wouldn't always be admitted, needless to say, and half the time he couldn't remember why, the events of the night before and the identities of those he had insulted or fought with lodged somewhere in the depths of his psyche, never to be recalled.

The man who had so recently been a hero in these self-same pubs was now an exile from them, like Napoleon in Elba, vaguely wondering why his world was collapsing round his feet. He was still, however, able to laugh off that fact just as quickly as the drink worked its schizoid magic on him.

He sought out contentious scenarios in which to exorcise his frustrations, and to exhibit his bile. Before too long, however, his myth preceded him and the manner in which shadow melted into substance eventually proved his undoing. There's a story Pronsias MacAonghusa tells about visiting him in hospital one time where Behan, who was to have been interviewed by MacAonghusa, simply said to him: 'Look, you sit down and read the papers, and I'll write down all the funny things I'm supposed to have said. I know what the crowd want.'

This is reminiscent of the comments Malcolm Muggeridge made after Behan had been drunk on his TV show: 'There was a crafty, calculating side to Behan. After his drunken appearance on my TV programme, the papers were full of him. He realised that one speechless TV appearance brought more of the things he wanted, like money and a neon glory about his head, than any number of hours with a pen in his hand.' J.P. Donleavy, in similar vein, claims he remembers a day when, after he had complimented Behan on a new suit he was wearing, Behan promptly went outside to the street and rolled himself around on the ground like a pig until it was well and truly ragged.

Behan needed few excuses to drink during his short life. He left Ireland to drink and he returned to it to drink. He drank when he was up and drank when he was down and when he wasn't sure if he was up or down, he drank to find out. He had many rationalisations for this, perhaps the most amusing one contained in *Brendan Behan's Island*, where a character says: 'Milk interferes with my digestion. I'd be going against my doctor's orders if I drank it. I'd be going against my religion if I drank tea or coffee, and I'm just about to have something to eat, and I need something to drink with my food.'

He hated being fêted as a raconteur when his writing wasn't going well, or when the juices or inspiration weren't flowing, but – either due to personal insecurities or the adrenaline rush of the booze – he went along with the charade as a kind of freak side-show to his literary career. In time, however, the two became inextricable, creating him in the guise of a rollicking wit who lived up to that image with alacrity, even when he had to be carried out of pubs on stretchers.

After it was discovered that Behan was also suffering from diabetes, his drink options were severely curtailed. Now there was a dietary complication, and if he failed to abide by it, or if he was away from Beatrice, who was beginning to lose control of him, he was liable to fall into a coma if he over-indulged. The diabetes was also responsible for his cantankerous mood-swings when under the influence. Behan knew he was walking a greased tightrope, and worried about it, but sometimes he was too drunk – or convulsed – to care. It was all part of a dreadful spiral leading to only one inevitable outcome.

Things nearly came to that particular pass towards the end of 1963 when, celebrating the birth of his daughter Blanaid, he lapsed into precisely that diabetic coma. He was also suffering from hepatitis, and on Christmas Day received the Last Rites. He made a near-miraculous recovery on that occasion, but a month later the newspapers again had him on their front pages, for he was found on a roadside not far from his house in a pool of blood. Nobody knew how he got there or what had happened to him, least of all Behan.

Three months later, sitting in a bar with his mother, he found himself succumbing to inexplicable sweats and chills, and he was taxied to hospital. It was to be the beginning of the end for the great man, for this time he didn't rally. He died that night – probably as the result of a bottle of brandy a visitor from England had smuggled in to him.

The turn-out at his funeral emulated that of Michael Collins or Parnell, resembling more the removal of a stage dignitary's remains than those of somebody who was, at the end of the day, a minor writer. The mourners came from every walk of life, but the only people Behan would really like to have seen there were his own: the working class faithful. The middle classes, he had often complained 'put years on me'.

As one writer put it, 'Flanked by his IRA comrades and followed by his friends, his funeral had honoured places for the gurriers, the bowsies, the ould wans and the chisellers. The people he had loved laid their laughing boy in

Glasnevin, at peace finally with the sycophantic world which had destroyed him.'

A sadder fact by far, as Ted Boyle remarked in his biography of him, was that by the time Behan died, his reputation as a writer had been almost completely overshadowed by his near-rabelaisian antics in bars. As Boyle put it, 'His reputation was much like that of a dog whose master had taught him to play checkers. The dog did not win many games, but the fact that he could play at all was amazing. When Behan died, people generally did not remark about the passing of a great writer, but about the death of a famous drunk who also wrote a bit.' The cause of death was listed as fatty degeneration of the liver, but as Boyle states, it might just as easily have been called suicide, 'for Behan's manner of dying was only nominally different from Hemingway's or Van Gogh's'.

We remember him today for his roguish wiles, his gap-toothed smile, his endless ribaldry with those who elevated him to quasi-mythic status only to delight in tearing him down again, but most of all for his heart-warming wit and blithe absence of anything approaching literary snobbery or self-importance. A streetwise character who will perhaps be remembered by posterity for most of the wrong reasons, he did however leave a body of work that has stood the test of time. The fact that his own turbulent personality is splattered over most of it in blood, sweat and tears is both his genius and his tragedy.

Behan on Behan

I'm not a communist. I'm too humble and modest. The communist want to free all the workers of the world. I'm content to make a start and free one member of it at a time ... myself.
Brendan Behan's Island, 1962

We're all good kids. We're all the kids our mothers warned us against.
Borstal Boy, 1958

I am married to a very dear girl who is an artist. We have no children except me.
Brendan Behan, 1970

I could become a South Californian phoney, live on black molasses and wind up in Santa Monica.
Monterey Pen Herald, 1961

If there were only three Irish people left in the world, you'd find two of them in a corner talking about the other one. We're a backbiting race. But if the third man happened to be Brendan Behan, he'd be away in a corner singing, writing, shouting and swearing at the other two.
The Wit of Brendan Behan, 1968

The Sayings of Brendan Behan

I'm not a war-like man. In fact I'm a highly ineffectual one. The IRA had sufficient military sense to never make me more than a messenger boy.

Confessions of an Irish Rebel, 1965

I was related to an Alsatian by marriage.

Hold Your Hour and Have Another, 1963

My grandmother and Miss McCann liked me more than any other kid I knew. I like being liked, and could only admire their taste.

Brendan Behan's Island, 1962

If it's a thing I go in for in a human being, it's weakness. I'm a divil for it.

Hold Your Hour and Have Another, 1963

I am not a priest but a sinner. I am not a psychiatrist but a neurotic. My neuroses are the nails and saucepans by which I get my living. If I were cured, I would have to go back to house-painting.

Brendan Behan's New York, 1964

When I'm talking to people I like to stop and quote myself. My quotes have a way of spicing up a conversation.

With Brendan Behan, 1981

I was reared a pet, God love me.

Hold Your Hour and Have Another, 1963

I have a mind that would burst rather than sustain a mood or a subject for long.

Man and Showman, 1966

I'd like to be a rich communist.

Newsweek, 1961

As my mother once remarked, anything that would shock Brendan Behan would turn thousands grey.

Confessions of an Irish Rebel, 1965

I am allergic to painting. Not to paint, mind you, but to putting the stuff on.

Ibid.

I am a sociable worker.

The Hostage, 1958

Since I was sixteen I've been in jails and Borstal institutions. I don't regret my time in England. IRA prisoners in Ireland, I've discovered, are an uninteresting and boring lot.

The World of Brendan Behan, 1965

I was no country Paddy from the middle of the Bog of Allen to be frightened to death by a lot of Liverpool seldom-fed bastards, nor was I one of your wrap-the-green-flag-around-me junior Civil Servants that came into the IRA from the Gaelic league, and well ready to die for their country any day of the week, purity in their hearts, truth on their lips, for the glory of God and the honour of Ireland. No, be Jesus, I was from Russell Street, North Circular Road, Dublin, from the Northside, where, be Jesus, the whole of this pack of Limeys and scruff-hounds, would be et, bet and threw up again – et without salt.

Borstal Boy, 1958

The Sayings of Brendan Behan

Whistler, the English painter, remarked that the world was divided into two classes: invalids and nurses. I'm a nurse.

> From an interview with Eamonn Andrews,
> quoted in the *Evening Press*, 1964

I'm a bad Catholic. It's the religion of all great artists.

> *Ibid.*

I always get grateful and pious in good weather.

> *Borstal Boy*, 1958

If I'm a snob I'm a working class snob, and that's the best kind.

> *My Life with Brendan*, 1973

I'm a Caucasian according to American standards; a European by promotion – and an Irishman by a stroke of bloody good luck.

> *The Wit of Brendan Behan*, 1968

I have a sense of humour that would nearly cause me to burst out laughing at a funeral, providing it was not my own.

> *Borstal Boy*, 1958

I respect kindness to human beings first of all, and kindness to animals. I don't respect the law. I have a total irreverence for anything connected with society except that which makes the roads safer, the beer stronger, the food cheaper and old men and old women warmer in winter and happier in summer.

> From the jacket of *Borstal Boy*, US edition

Behan on Others

Other people have a nationality. The Irish and the Jews have a *psychosis*.
Richard's Cork Leg, 1973

The only man I ever heard admitting he was a Black and Tan was a Liverpool lad who said he joined up because he hadn't the fare for the Foreign Legion!
The Wit of Brendan Behan, 1968

They try to live up to the reputation all taxi drivers have, of being a wit. As I am in the wit business myself, I object to competition.
On New York Taxi drivers, from
Brendan Behan's New York, 1964

They put years on me. If they didn't see my name in the *Sunday Times* and the *Observer*, they wouldn't want to know me.
On the middle classes, from
Brendan Behan's Island, 1962

An Anglo-Irishman only works at riding horses, drinking whiskey and reading double-meaning jokes at Trinity College.
The Hostage, 1958

My grandmother took a bath every year, whether she was dirty or not.
Brendan Behan's Island, 1962

He was born English, and remained so for years.
The Hostage, 1958

Pat: He was an Anglo-Irishman.
Meg: In the blessed name of God, what's that?
Pat: A Protestant with a horse.
Ibid.

It must be the best-fed company in the whole of Europe, because every time the action slacks, they eat something. You can't get away with that in revue.
On the Abbey Theatre Company, from *With Brendan Behan*, 1981

He's a great skin, and he kept me going with occasional hand-outs when my readies were low. I don't understand his plays, but so what? I go for swims in the ocean, and I don't understand that either.
On Samuel Beckett, *ibid.*

Writers & Writing

If you get six out of six good reviews, you can ask the President of the United States to sell you The White House, but I don't think this has ever happened. If you get 5 out of 6, you're still doing fairly well, though you have to start worrying then about 480 Lexington Avenue (the tax base). 4 good reviews means you can throw a party, and even afford to attend it too! 3 means it's time to go home to bed, but if you only get 2 you're best to stay there all day and don't show your face in public till after dark. If you get just one good view from six, make an air reservation. And if you get none ... take a sleeping pill.
Brendan Behan's New York, 1964

How the hell can I write the way Irishmen talk if I don't use the F word? After all, that effer Lawrence got away with it.
The Wit of Brendan Behan, 1968

An author's first duty is to let down his country.
Guardian, 1960

I was one time arguing a person who writes plays and he said to me, 'My plays will be remembered when you're dead and rotten.' Well I said, 'I want to tell you something. Number one, I'm not interested in having my plays remembered when I'm dead and rotten, and number two, I'm not particularly attracted by the idea of being dead and rotten anyway!'
Evening Press, 1964

The Sayings of Brendan Behan

Besides being a colourless unimaginative writer and an obvious degenerate, he should have been hanged, drawn and quartered for desecrating valuable paper with his muck.

On James Joyce, from
With Brendan Behan, 1981

In certain circumstances a sow shown on stage having a litter of piglets could be classed as high art, provided it had the right author.

A Memoir, 1985

If my plays show anything, it is that no ideal is worth the shedding of one drop of human blood.

Attributed

I'm driven to writing by murophobia: the fear of having to paint walls. I don't know if the pen is mightier than the sword, but it's definitely lighter than the brush.

Vogue, 1956

Richard's Cork Leg isn't a drama or a comedy – it's a dramedy.

Manchester Evening News, 1961

Its impact was like the banging together of two damp dish-cloths.

On a play he disliked. *Attributed*

The key to reading *Ulysses* is to treat it like a comedian would – as a sort of glorified gag book.

Attributed

Writers & Writing

I write about the people I know. I record how they talk and act and how they smell, with liquor and stale sour sweat coming out of their pores.
Washington Post, 1964

I don't know many working writers in Ireland at the moment because there *aren't* any. There are civil servants, spoiled priests waiting to be rehabilitated, judges, ex-convicts, retired nuns and escaped agriculturists who write: but these are only honorary *screevenorai* (writers).
Brendan Behan's Island, 1962

I didn't lick me words from the bricks of Dublin.
With Brendan Behan, 1981

How can any writer attack another man's fatherland if he doesn't attack his own first?
New York Times, 1960

The trouble with that lot of bastards is that they're illiterate. They've never blue-pencilled anything I've done in Gaelic because they couldn't *read* it.
On the Censorship Board, after they banned *Borstal Boy,* quoted in *Newsweek,* 1959

When Beckett was in Trinity College listening to lectures, I was in the Queen's Theatre. That is why my plays are music hall, and his are university lectures.
A Memoir, 1985

They go on forever ... about nothing.
On newspapers, from *Man and Showman,* 1966

The Sayings of Brendan Behan

I don't see why a writer should be cohesive, any more than plumbers or bankers should be cohesive.
Brendan Behan's New York, 1964

Whoever writes my biography will get no help from my letters. I never write any.
A Memoir, 1985

Journalism is the last refuge of the literary mediocre.
Confessions of an Irish Rebel, 1965

One of the reasons I never write letters is that I can get more than a dollar a word for writing literature.
Letter to Rory Furlong, 1961

Cultural activity in present-day Dublin is largely agricultural. They write mostly about their hungry bogs and the great scarcity of crumpet. I am a city rat. Joyce is dead and O'Casey is in Devon. The people writing here now have as much interest in me as an epic poet in Finnish, or a Lapland novelist.
Brendan Behan, 1970

The cat in No. 70 will be writing next.
To his father, after hearing his brother Brian had written his memoirs, *ibid.*

(Sean) O'Casey is like champagne, one's wedding night, or the Aurora Borealis.
Brendan Behan's Island, 1962

Writers & Writing

I never went to a play except to be entertained, and sometimes even left the theatre before the third act had got under way in the pursuit of drink.

Brendan Behan, 1970

I couldn't be bothered with Joyce or any of that jazz.

Sunday Telegraph, 1961

I'm a writer. I've never seen myself as anything else, not even from the age of 6 when my mother says she sent me for a loaf of bread and I used to kick a piece of paper along the street in front of me so that I could read it.

Confessions of an Irish Rebel, 1965

There's more where that came from, as the mother of twenty said.

In a letter to Iain Hamilton, after submitting *Borstal Boy* to him, 1958

I've always thought T.S. Eliot wasn't far wrong when he said that the main problem for the dramatist today is to keep his audience amused; and that while they were laughing their heads off, you could be up to any bloody thing behind their backs – and it was what you were doing behind their bloody backs that made your play great.

Confessions of an Irish Rebel, 1965

I didn't write this play. The lags wrote it.

After the opening night of *The Quare Fellow*, from *Brendan Behan* by Ted Boyle, 1969

God dammit, you might as well be out of this world as out of the fashion, for didn't Joyce and O'Casey have their plays rejected one time?

> Reaction to the rejection of *The Quare Fellow* by the Abbey Theatre, from *Confessions of an Irish Rebel*, 1965

If the Mycenaean poets could do it, then so can I. I do not set myself up as an authority on these matters, but if Homer is to be believed, the Greeks wrote their books by improvising them in talk.

> Justifying his decision to speak his later books into tape recorders rather than write them, quoted in *Man and Showman*, 1966

The trouble with this (expletive deleted) writing is that you have to be by yourself while you're doing it. And that's hard.

> *Dead As Doornails*, 1976

Ireland & the Irish

I believe they manage things better across the other side. Sure God help the Irish, if it was raining soup, they'd be out with forks.
Brendan Behan's Island, 1962

It is said that the commander of a Japanese submarine that came to Cork was asked what he thought of it, and he replied that the only difficulty he and the crew had was in distinguishing one Corkman from another.
Hold Your Hour and Have Another, 1963

In Ireland, down the country anyway, if a girl got up the pole she might as well leave on the next boat or drown herself and have done with it. The people there are so Christian and easily shocked.

Borstal Boy, 1958

Ken: Some people don't like the Irish. I do.
Brendan: We're very popular among ourselves.
Ibid.

He was an Irishman of the variety best known to me, who would be happily absorbed in the problem of seeing who he could 'do' next.
Confessions of an Irish Rebel, 1965

'Are you Irish?'
'No,' I said. 'As a matter of fact I'm a Yemenite Arab!'
Ibid.

The Sayings of Brendan Behan

The Irish are not my audience; they are my raw material.
> *Evening Press*, 1964

It's not that the Irish are cynical. It's rather that they have a wonderful lack of respect for everything and everybody.
> *Globe and Mail*, 1961

The Irish who fought for that fascist Franco at least had the good sense to come home with more men than they went out with.
> *With Brendan Behan*, 1981

An Irishman is never at peace unless he's fighting.
> *Joys of Irish Humour*, 1978

Frankly, I don't give two hoots what impression I give. Nobody ever paid me anything for being Irish.
> *The People*, 1961

For some reason, the old fellow who has been to America is better thought of than the one who has only got as far as Liverpool. I think they must sit up with maps, measuring the distance so as to know to what honours the returning exile is entitled.
> On Irish people's attitude to emigrants, from *Hold Your Hour and Have Another*, 1963

The only crime he ever committed was having three plays running simultaneously in the West End.
> On Oscar Wilde, from *With Brendan Behan*, 1981

Ireland & the Irish

The Irish are so chauvinistic, they'll even accept *me*.

Globe and Mail, 1961

Officer: The loss of liberty is a terrible thing.
Pat: That's not the worst thing. Nor the redcaps, nor the screws. Do you know what the worst thing is?
Officer: No.
Pat: The other Irish patriots in along with you.

The Hostage, 1958

Some time ago there was a famine in this country and people were dying all over the place. Well your Queen Victoria, or whatever her bloody name was, sent £5 to the Famine Relief Fund, and at the same time she sent £5 to the Battersea Dog's Home so no one could accuse her of having rebel sympathies.

Ibid.

'Tell me, ma'am,' he says, 'do you know the names of these three islands out there?'
'I couldn't tell you, sir,' she said. 'They weren't there when I'd gone to bed last night.'

Brendan Behan's Island, 1962

I like living in Dublin because there my enemies are all about and it's very cosy.

Herald Tribune, 1959

Irish is more direct than English, more bitter. It's a muscular fine thing, the most expansive language in Europe.

Brendan Behan's Island, 1962

I've never seen a native of Blarney kiss the Blarney stone – I suppose they don't have to.
Ibid.

They only call me when they hear that I'm in hospital, in some jail, or about to die.
On the Irish media, from *With Brendan Behan*, 1981

The only thing I ever had in common with Blythe was that I could tell him to fuck off in Irish.
On his *bête noire* Ernest Blythe, sometime director of the Abbey Theatre, from *A Memoir*, 1985

Other Nationalities

Somebody said the Swedes have the highest suicide rate in the world, but that's rubbish. The reason they have a high rate is because they give the statistics, whereas in England or Ireland if somebody croaks themselves they say, 'Oh, he didn't know the gun was loaded,' or, 'He didn't know that seven million aspirins could knock you off.'

Brendan Behan's New York, 1964

The two things they worship the most have both, oddly enough, Greek names – the telephone and the television. I think without any disrespect to the Catholic Church, that this should be their religion instead of Roman Catholicism, because nobody has ever heard of Romanvision or Romanphone.

On American teenagers, *ibid.*

They boast of the heartlessness of the multitude, and how a man could lie in Times Square for a month without anyone going near him, except to rob or rape him.

On Americans in general, *ibid.*

The English and Americans dislike only some Irish, the same Irish that the Irish themselves detest – the ones that think.

Richard's Cork Leg, 1973

The Sayings of Brendan Behan

The English are wonderful. First they put me in jail, and then they made me rich.

Attributed

It will be a fine town, when it's finished.

Of Toronto, attributed

I have never, in my travels, met anyone worse than myself. I know there are some hardchaws among them, though. In fact I would much rather see the tinkers fall out at the fair of Aughrim than watch an Arab row.

Hold Your Hour and Have Another, 1963

There are three things I don't like about New York: the water, the buses and the professional Irishmen. A professional Irishman is one who is terribly anxious to pass as a middle-class Englishman.

Daily News, 1961

English Catholics had no time for the Irish except when they were begging from them. They had no use for Paddy the navvy or Biddy the skivvy, beyond taking their money when a new church was being built.

Borstal Boy, 1958

It's for nothing. You could wash your feet in it.

On Spanish beer, from *My Life with Brendan,* 1973

The best way to get a proper accent in the Irish or Hebrew language is to go to Central Park on a cold winter's morning and listen to a taxi-man clearing his throat.

Brendan Behan's New York, 1964

Other Nationalities

America is the richest country in the world. Why can't you afford at least one free television show where they don't over-burden a man with all those (expletive deleted) commercials?
Philadelphia TV Guide, 1961

The more I see of the Canadians on Fleet Street, the more I like the Limeys.
Globe and Mail, 1961

The sort of man many American women want to marry is the fellow with a will of his own ... preferably made out in her favour.
The Wit of Brendan Behan, 1968

The British are a gentle race – at least when you take away their guns, their queens and their kings.
The World of Brendan Behan, 1965

It's a city everyone should live in when they're young or very old. It's no place for the middle-aged. But then, where the hell *is?*
On Paris, from 'The Meanjin Quarterly', 1968

New York is a fabulous place. The whole population, all 20 million of them, should be investigated by a committee for being so jolly.
Man and Showman, 1966

There's more difference between a Manchester man and a London man than there is between a Belfast man and a Dublin man.
Brendan Behan's Island, 1962

There's many a good heart beats under a khaki tunic.
The Hostage, 1958

There is everything to fit an Irishman in France. He can even find a good Irish excuse for getting into any political argument there.
Confessions of an Irish Rebel, 1965

Everyone has their own way of looking at things and you couldn't blame (the English) for taking a favourable view of their own kicking once they were kicking you in their own country and not being kicked by someone else in someone else's.
Borstal Boy, 1958

Only a deaf mute could be raised by my mother and be unable to catalogue England's misdemeanours from Africa backwards.
Attributed

A few weeks ago in Toronto a Canadian said that it was an awful black eye for the Yanks that the Russians had put a spaceman up before the Americans. I said to him, 'My friend, Ireland will put up a shillelagh into orbit, Israel will put a matzo ball into orbit, and Lichtenstein will put a postage stamp into orbit before you Canadians ever put up a mouse.'
Brendan Behan, 1970

The famed British reserve is as much a myth as the idea of the broth-of-a-boy Irishman, he of the ready wit and the warm heart and the great love for a fight.
Hold Your Hour and Have Another, 1963

Other Nationalities

Lenin said that communism is socialism with electricity. New York is Paris with the English language.

Brendan Behan, 1970

I go to New York for spiritual regeneration. When I arrive here from Canada, I am so grateful that I am in the United States that even Howard Johnson's architecture in Buffalo cheers me up.

Ibid.

The man that hates the United States hates the human race.

Attributed

Alcohol

When pressed, I will even drink with nobility.
Confessions of an Irish Rebel, 1965

Alcoholics die of alcohol, don't they?
To his doctor Terence Chapman, quoted in
Interviews and Recollections, 1982

I never turned to drink. It seemed to turn to me.
Evening Press, 1964

I never gargle on the job. Water is the only formula for writing.
Irish Press, 1964

I write in order to keep myself in liquor.
Newsweek, 1959

Why do I drink? Firstly, because I like the stuff. And secondly because I like company. Furthermore, I've been at it with my grandmother since I was six. By the time I was ten, I knew the taste of it better than tea.
Irish Digest, 1963

It's only when I have nothing to do that I hit the bottle.
Ibid.

I'm not proud of being an alcoholic, but neither am I going to apologise to anyone for being one.
Ibid.

Alcohol

The bars (in Dublin) are shut from 2.30 to 3.30. We call it the Holy Hour. The politician that introduced it in the Dail was shot an hour afterwards.
Sunday Express, 1958

I'm on the wagon. It's not easy to smile when you're drinking this stuff. I may need a stomach pump.
After being spotted with a bottle of milk in his hand, from *Brendan Behan*, 1970

The drink in that pub isn't fit for washing hearses.
Attributed

Hard-chaws, ex-convicts, chancers and tramps who'd lift the froth off your pint if you didn't keep your nose well in over the edge of the glass.
On the company he tended to meet in bars, from *The People*, 1959

Afterwards I really feel I've earned my breakfast – a large brandy and a plateful of benzedrine.
On why he loved early morning swims, from *Remembering How We Stood*, 1987

The trouble with me is that I should be drinking stout all the time, but I can afford spirits.
A Memoir, 1985

The Sayings of Brendan Behan

For a start let me tell you that I am neither dead, drunk nor dotty. I'm just damn sick, but getting better all the time. My liver, I'm told, is like the sole of a hobnailed boot. My inside feels as if it has been scoured out with sulphuric acid, and my head occasionally thumps like a pneumatic drill.

> On his medical condition after a stay in hospital, from *Brendan Behan,* 1970

Ebbing and flowing. Ebbing in the morning and flowing at night.

> On being asked how he intended to spend New Year's Eve, from *The Wit of Brendan Behan,* 1968

Only twice a day – when I'm thirsty and when I'm not.

> When asked how often he drank, *ibid.*

They don't apparently care about people being drunk in the Navy, which is uncommon civil of them, and to their lasting credit.

> *Brendan Behan's Island* 1962

If I had my way, I'd cut it all out and give my head a break for the killer thoughts that are in it.

> *Man and Showman,* 1966

The only thing I envy young people is their livers.

> *Brendan Behan,* 1970

I sometimes feel terrible, but don't know what the trouble is, so have another drink.

> *Daily Mail,* 1959

Alcohol

When I was growing up, being drunk was not regarded as a disgrace. To have enough to eat was regarded as an achievement, and drunkenness as a victory.

Evening Press, 1964

Whatever you say, Bill, whatever you say. But I'll just have one more to wash down the last one.

To John B. Keane's son Billy, who had just implored him not to have another drink, from *The Real Keane*, 1992

Fame & the Media

It's damn near killing me. I think a man should be allowed success for one month, and then given a pension and allowed to retire.
Man and Showman, 1966

I don't know why my books sell, but if people are willing to pay nearly a pound for them, well it shows they're not merely doing so because they heard I was drunk on television.
Attributed

Anytime I want to go on TV, all I do is say the word and I get a fistful of dollars. Not bad for a working class boy from the bog.
With Brendan Behan, 1981

I look like anyone else when I'm sober, but when I have a few inside me I look interesting. That's when the photographers get out their cameras to take pictures of the Wild Boyo, and when they start scratching down in their note-books all the idiocies that any man is capable of in his cups. It's Brendan the drunk they've come to see, not Brendan the writer. Yet every word I've ever written has been set down when I was sober.
Manchester Evening News, 1961

I'd rather be famous than a f***ing house-painter.
Monterey Peninsula Herald, 1961

Fame & the Media

There is nothing that annoys me more than people who try to put a tag on generations of writers, as if all writing was done in a maternity hospital.
Brendan Behan's New York, 1964

When I go for my tea, people break into print about me.
With Brendan Behan, 1981

They only call me when they hear that I'm in a hospital, in some jail, or about to die.
On the Irish media, *ibid.*

There's no such thing as bad publicity except your own obituary.
My Brother Brendan, 1965

I go to better beds ... but I sleep less well.
On the effect of fame, from *Man and Showman*, 1966

Sure if I took notice of my critics, I'd be in Grangegorman [a mental home] long ago.
The Real Keane, 1992

Fame is failure disguised as money.
The Irish Digest, 1963

Religion

Philosophically, I'm a daylight atheist. However, when I'm ill I try to find a priest. You might say I live by a calculated cowardice.

Herald Tribune, 1962

I don't want to push my luck. My interest in the next life is purely academic.

When he finally realised his
drinking was life-threatening,
from *Newsweek*, 1961

The great majority of Irish people believe that if you become a priest or a nun, you've a better chance of going to heaven. If it's a virtue to meditate in a monastery and get food and shelter for doing it, why then isn't it a virtue outside? I'm a lay contemplative.

A Paler Shade of Green, 1972

The day the Catholic and Protestant churches combine, it's the end of all drinking. I'll have to go to Rome to sabotage the affair.

Newsweek, 1959

I have nothing against the church, as long as they leave the drink alone.

Ibid.

'Anything in the paper this morning, Julia?'
'Nothing, Mary. Only the Pope is trying to make peace.'
'God forgive him. It's a wonder he wouldn't mind his own interference. It's enough to make you turn Protestant.'
Brendan Behan's Island, 1962

They used to have religious texts on the walls of the condemned cell in Durham. One of them said, 'Today is the morrow you worried about yesterday.' It was the last thing a bloke saw as he went out to be hanged.
Borstal Boy, 1958

Blasphemy is merely the comic verse of belief.
New York Times, 1960

Begod, there was a million Irish pilgrims going through Paris on their way to Lourdes. I suppose they wanted to see a bit of wickedness before they got caught up in the blazin' fervour of their religion. But they were a miserable hungry lot. It was terrible hard work to get the price of a drink or a bit of bread and cheese outa them. All their effin' charity must have been reserved for buyin' candles at the shrines.
Me Darlin' Dublin's Dead and Gone, 1983

I want to die when I'm ninety with a mountain of pillows behind me, and sixty priests and forty nuns praying fervently I will go to heaven.
The Wit of Brendan Behan, 1968

The Behans have always been Catholics and anti-clerical. None of us became a priest, but everyone is dying for clerical help. I wish God were for hire.
L'Express, 1959

I'm a bad Catholic. It's the religion of great artists.
Interviews and Recollections, 1982

Only dirty people have to wash. It's like the Sacrament of Penance. When I'm asked if I've been to confession recently, I always answer, 'No, that's only for sinners.'
Confessions of an Irish Rebel, 1982

I'd prefer to be dead than to think about death.
Daily Telegraph, 1961

The Bible was a consolation to a fellow alone in the old cell. The lovely thin paper and a bit of mattress in it – if you could get a match – was as good a smoke as I ever tasted.
The Quare Fellow, 1956

He was a genuine religious man and one of the few religious men that was not a worse bastard than ordinary people.
After The Wake, 1981

God gives us the brains. It's no credit to ourselves.
The Hostage, 1958

Religion

Mrs Mallarkey: Perhaps you don't know what a pervert is.
Cronin: I do. I read biographies.
Bawd: A pervert is when a Catholic becomes a Protestant.
The Hero: Not a pervert. A convert.
Bawd: A convert is when a Protestant becomes a Catholic.
The Hero: In England, a pervert is a man who has sex relations with other men.
Cronin: Well I might have a go at that too.

Richard's Cork Leg, 1973

> The bells of hell
> Go ting-a-ling-a-ling
> For you but not for me.
> Oh death where is thy
> Sting-a-ling-a-ling
> Or grave thy victory?
> If you meet the undertaker
> Or the young man from the Pru
> Get a pint of what's left over
> Now I'll say goodbye to you.
>
> *The Hostage*, 1958

I regard the next world as a place full of foreigners.   *Herald Tribune*, 1959

Even when the drink takes to me, I find that when darkness falls, I think of my prayers.
Sunday Express, 1960

You must understand that politics to me is a second religion.   *Sunday Independent*, 1964

Thank you, Sister. May you be the mother of a bishop!
> To a nun nursing him on his deathbed,
> attributed

The way some civil servants talk, you'd think God was in another department.
> *The Wit of Brendan Behan*, 1968

The middle and upper classes use a show called the Orange Order for keeping the working classes in line. Any time they show signs of getting out of hand and looking for a bigger cut of the joint, some religious issue is raised and the Orange Order calls everyone out for the defence of their ancient freedoms against the imaginary onslaughts of the Papists.
> *Hold Your Hour and Have Another*, 1963

Them that have all the talk about how nice it is in the next world, I don't see any great hurry on them getting on there.
> *Ibid.*

Our church is not for hypocrites, it's for sinners as well as saints, and one mortal sin is as good or as bad as another, whether it was against the Sixth and Ninth Commandment or the Fifth and Tenth.
> *Borstal Boy*, 1958

I had been extra religious as a kid, and the day I made my First Communion I had prayed to God to take me, as Napoleon prayed, when I would go straight to heaven.
> *Ibid.*

Insults

The best thing I can say about bagpipes is that they don't smell too.
Hold Your Hour and Have Another, 1963

Why should I lend my good name to that shower of hypocrites and blatherskites? Did they ever do anything for the working class people of Ireland?
Upon declining to attend the John F. Kennedy Inauguration ball, from *With Brendan Behan,* 1981

The only brigade you'd be fit for is the fire brigade.
To a man who claimed to have been in the same IRA brigade as himself, from *The Real Keane,* 1992

People who are compelled to abandon their homelands in search of a better way of life are troglodytes and low class scum. I'm here at the invitation of Hollywood moguls and Broadway producers.
With Brendan Behan, 1981

They're like eunuchs in a harem. They're at the theatre every night, they see how it *should* be done, but they can't do it themselves.
On critics, attributed

The Sayings of Brendan Behan

The Governor was a desiccated-looking man, in tweed clothes and wearing a cap, as befitted his rank of Englishman, and looking as if he would ride a horse if he had one.

Borstal Boy, 1958

Considering the world is a madhouse, who better to patrol it than armed idiots?

On policemen, from *With Brendan Behan*, 1981

Unless you're a policeman, a criminal or a prostitute, you have no business there.

On Piccadilly, from *Brendan Behan's New York*, 1964

The main function phonies provide is that of standing struggling artists a drink.

Ibid.

Chairman Mao Tse Tung will soon put a stop to your f***ing gallop, ye creepin' Jesus's ye.

To a group of carol singers who were annoying him one Christmas, from *Dead As Doornails*, 1976

They should all be taken out and shot. There has to be better ways to line coffins.

On folk singers, from *With Brendan Behan*

Franco's funeral!

Upon being asked what he would most like to witness during his stay in Spain, from *The Wit of Brendan Behan*, 1968

Insults

He had a face like a plateful of mortal sins.
> *Hold Your Hour and Have Another*, 1964

He's the only one of the Burkes who can write. I mean his *name*.
> Of his co-author cousin Jimmy Burke,
> from *Smile and Be a Villain*, 1995

I think they burn the chairs at these because apparently they don't feel that a chair is a proper place to sit when listening to one of those groaners.
> On folk sessions, from *Brendan Behan's New York*, 1964

I entered a raffle once where the first prize was a week in Belfast and the second prize *two* weeks in Belfast.
> Attributed

I now have a theory on what happened to the snakes when St Patrick drove them out of Ireland. They all came to New York and became judges.
> *Newsweek*, 1961

The Fianna Fáil crowd recognised but the one true Pope, by the name of Eamon de Valera, late of 42nd Street.
> *After the Wake*, 1981

I hate the Reds generally. They are snobbish and ill-mannered and if you haven't got a job and aren't looking for one, they have no time for you.
> *Confessions of an Irish Rebel*, 1965

People don't actually swim in Dublin Bay.
They're merely going through the motions.
Attributed

Limerick is the city of piety and shiety.
More Kicks Than Pence, 1992

Pat: Is he a policeman?
Teresa: Oh no, sir, he looks respectable.
The Hostage, 1958

> Come in you Anglo-Saxon swine
> and drink of my Algerian wine
> 'Twill turn your eyeballs black and blue
> and darn well good enough for you
>
> A message he scrawled on a Parisian café window
> to attract the attention of English-speaking
> tourists, from *My Life With Brendan*, 1973

Tom: Have you noticed nearly all thieves are Tories?
Brendan: Maybe it's because all Tories are thieves.
Borstal Boy, 1958

You're the life and soul of the party, aren't you? You remind me of the little girl who was sent in to cheer her father up. She was so good at it that he cut his throat.
The Quare Fellow, 1956

Dunlavin: Do you know who feels it worse going out to be topped?
Prisoner A: Corkmen and Northerners. They've such bloody hard necks.
Ibid.

Insults

Teresa: I've always heard that De Valera is a wonderful man. They say he's fluent in seven languages.
Patrick: More's the pity we can't understand him once in a while.

The Hostage, 1958

I never came across a situation so dismal that a policeman couldn't make it worse.

On New York's *'Open End'* show in 1959

Ratface was about the ugliest server I'd ever seen, and a real cup-of-tea Englishman with a mind the width of his back garden that'd skin a black man, providing he'd get another to hold him, and send the skin 'ome to mum.

Borstal Boy, 1958

Money

The number of people who buy books in Ireland wouldn't keep me in drink for the duration of a Sunday opening-time.
My Life With Brendan, 1973

To hell with poverty – we'll kill a chicken.
Brendan Behan, 1970

If people want me to behave like Cardinal Spellman or Billy Graham, why don't they pay me the salary these fellows are getting.
The World of Brendan Behan, 1965

I was making better money as a bricklayer. Pity to God I ever gave it up.
Remembering How We Stood, 1987

They've banned *Borstal Boy*, but they don't mind taking my money. They object to my tainted books, but not to my tainted cash.
My Life With Brendan, 1973

To supplement some ignoramus in the Government who couldn't tell a pit from a rabbit.
Upon being asked why he was going to America, *ibid.*

Pound notes is the best religion in the world.
The Hostage, 1958

Wit

Incense is a kind of smoke with perfume in it.
Borstal Boy, 1958

I'm a playwright, not a bloody postman.
To Colin MacInnes of the *Daily Telegraph* after being asked about the messages in his plays

I believe with Lenin that the main object of all political activity should be the abolition of the village idiot.
Brendan Behan's Island, 1962

A city is a place where you're least likely to get a bite from a wild sheep.
Ibid.

That I've celebrated my 86th birthday.
After being asked what he would like said of him in thirty years' time, from the *Evening Press*, 1964

Monsewer: A race occurs when a lot of people live in one place for a long period of time.
Soldier: I reckon our old sergeant major must be a race; he's been stuck in the same depot for about 40 years.
The Hostage, 1958

So many people belonging to me lay buried in Kilbarrack, the healthiest graveyard in Ireland, they said, because it was so near the sea.
Borstal Boy, 1958

Granny Growl: Me tired husband, poor ould Paddins, he was shot in the Dardanelles.
Granny Grunt: And a most painful part of the body to be shot!
Brendan Behan's Island, 1962

Well if I had to choose between Michaelangelo's David and Whistler's mother ...
After being asked if he was gay, from *Joan's Book*, 1994

You'd get them on the back of a postage stamp and still have room for the Koran.
On his brother Brian's proposed memoirs, quoted in *The Irish Press*, 1990

Violence

I'm a painter, you know, just like Hitler. But I'm not starting any wars. I've had enough of them.
Me Darlin' Dublin's Dead and Gone, 1983

There's no truth in the Dublin saying that when a Corkman starts calling you 'oul son' it's too late to look for the knife in your back.
Brendan Behan's Island, 1962

I was court-martialled in my absence and sentenced to death in my absence, so I said they could shoot me in my absence.
The Hostage, 1958

I served a sentence for attempting to murder two policemen – but by Jaysus, they weren't charged with a prior attempt to murder *me*.
The Wit of Brendan Behan, 1968

Isn't it better to be fightin' than to be lonely?
Hold Your Hour and Have Another, 1963

If you fight for the liberty and unity of a small country you're an anarchist, but if you go bombin' for a great power, you're a patriot.
North American Review, 1964

The IRA didn't take sides. We were neutral, in favour of the one side only – our own.
Ibid.

The Sayings of Brendan Behan

I won't fire at an Englishman until we've beaten this bastard Hitler.
Evening Press, 1964

Pat: Where the hell were you in 1916 when the real fighting was going on?
Meg: I wasn't born.
Pat: You're full of excuses!
The Hostage, 1958

My name is Brendan Behan. I came over here to fight for the Irish Workers and the small Farmer's Republic, for a full and free life for my fellow countrymen north and south, and for the removal of the baneful influence of British imperialism from Irish affairs.
Borstal Boy, 1958

I have discovered no better way of doing your work as a soldier of the Irish Republic than by getting drunk.
Confessions of an Irish Rebel, 1965

A bit of shooting takes your mind off your troubles – it takes your mind off the cost of living.
The Hostage, 1958

I've planted more bombs than you've had hot dinners, you pox bottles.
To two bomb disposal experts, from *Joan's Book*, 1994

Any man who shoots at a policeman at 14 yards and misses him, deserves a year for every yard he missed him by.
Confessions of an Irish Rebel, 1965

General Ruminations

Killing your wife is a natural thing that could happen to the best of us.
The Quare Fellow, 1956

What I have against beatniks is that they're always looking for a job – *my* job.
New York Times, 1960

My attitude to homosexuality is rather like that of the woman who, at the time of the trial of Oscar Wilde, said she didn't mind what they did, so long as they didn't do it in the street and frighten the horses.
Brendan Behan's New York, 1964

The most important things in life are to get something to eat, something to drink and someone to love you.
Weekend, 1968

The ordinariness of people is what is often extraordinary.
Ibid.

Every cripple has his way of walking.
Confessions of an Irish Rebel, 1965

A job is death without the dignity.
Ibid.

On average, a man in good health should not have his heart broken more than six times a year.
Brendan Behan's New York, 1964

The Sayings of Brendan Behan

One of the Fenian prisoners said the things you missed most in jail were babies, dogs and fires.
Borstal Boy, 1958

Life is a whole lot better than death, any day of the week.
The Quare Fellow, 1956

Love is the most damnable emotion of all.
Man and Showman, 1966

I think weddings is sadder than funerals, because they remind you of your own wedding. You can't be reminded of your own funeral because it hasn't happened. But weddings always make me cry.
Richard's Cork Leg, 1972

> Never throw stones at your mother
> You'll be sorry for it when she's dead
> Never throw stones at your mother
> Throw bricks at your father instead.
> *The Hostage,* 1958

Inside every fat man there's a thin man trying to get out.
Evening Press, 1964

My father was ruined by hygiene. He used to supply sawdust to public houses. Now the days of the big spitters are over.
Richard's Cork Leg, 1973

A day is a long time in the country.
Evening Herald, 1964

General Ruminations

You should have met my granny. She lived on tinned salmon, snuff and porter – and never got out of bed except for funerals.

The Irish Digest, 1960

A shut mouth will catch no flies.

Hold Your Hour and Have Another, 1963

I cannot understand why very small children, when swimming on your back, cannot get the idea of holding on to your shoulders rather than half strangling you by the firm pressure of baby hands on your windpipe.

Ibid.

I would much rather see the tinkers fall out of the fair of Aughrim than watch an Arab row.

Ibid.

Isn't the day very changeable? You wouldn't know what to pawn.

Ibid.

Good or bad, it's better to be criticised than ignored.

Ibid.

All the better, as the old one said when she was told that there was no tea, but only porter.

Ibid.

If we live through the winter, the divil wouldn't kill us in summer.

Borstal Boy, 1958

The only reason they call me is because I happen to have a reputation. If I was the local milkman, or some poor cunt flogging turf from the back of a donkey's cart, the whores wouldn't even stop to give me a light.

On his treatment by the press, from
With Brendan Behan, 1981

I am prepared to die, and, if necessary, for France, but not for *Air* France.

After his plane had been struck by lightning
on a flight from Paris, from *Remembering*
How We Stood, 1987

It's a queer world, God knows, but the best we have to be going on with.

Borstal Boy, 1958